CURSES

by

Nicola Morgan

Illustrated by Kevin Hopgood

First published in 2008 in Great Britain by
Barrington Stoke Ltd
18 Walker Street, Edinburgh, EH3 7LP

www.barringtonstoke.co.uk

ISBN: 978-1-84299-492-4

Printed in Great Britain by Bell & Bain Ltd

Contents

Chapter 1
What is a Curse?

A curse is like a magic spell. An evil spell. It says that something bad might happen. Today, we don't tend to go round putting curses on people, because we don't believe in magic. But people used to believe that curses had great power. Most people were very scared of them.

The word 'curse' may come from an old word meaning 'anger'. Some of the curses in this book sound very angry indeed!

In the past, different people have had different beliefs, but nearly everyone has believed in the power of curses. Today, more people understand the real science that makes things happen. So most people understand that curses are to do with stories and myths, not truth. If you know how science really works, you won't believe in magic.

We don't believe that putting a curse on someone can really work. Do we?

Well, it's strange but we often do still seem to believe that. In this book, you'll read about curses that some people think have power today. And you can find more amazing stories on the internet and in other books. You can make up your own mind which to believe. Keep your brain wide awake when you hear stories about curses – people who make curses want you to believe them. The whole point is to make you scared.

Can anyone make a curse?

Yes!

You might curse a person who had done something bad to you. Or you might put a curse on your stack of money or jewels, so a robber would be too scared to steal them. People who were scared of being killed might make a curse to punish anyone who tried to murder them. (Being killed by someone would make you very angry indeed, so the dead person's curse would be extra powerful.) Witches and gypsies were supposed to be very good at making strong curses, so you wouldn't want to upset them.

People also thought that they could be cursed by God (or whatever gods they believed in at that time). If you did something bad, and then a few weeks later you broke your leg, and then someone else in your family fell ill – people might say God had cursed your family.

So, curses were to protect or punish.

Quite useful, then? And a good way of making sure people didn't do bad things. (But, if you think about it, that didn't work – because people still did just as many bad things in the old days as they do today!)

How do you curse someone?

If you wanted to put a curse on someone planning to steal your money, you would write down some strong words. Then you would try to give these words a magic power. You would make the words as scary and horrible as you could. A witch or holy person might help you, or you might ask a god or evil spirit to come up with the best, most powerful magic words.

You might write, "I curse the man, woman or child who opens this box – may dogs rip him open and may maggots eat his eyes! May his guts be pecked by crows while he's still alive and may his nose be full of slimy worms!" A witch might tell you to do something, like spit on the words three times or drink a cup of bats' blood. Then if someone tried to steal the money, they would see the curse and read it, and be too scared to go ahead. Well, if you read those words, would you risk it?

Another way of making a curse is just to shout out the words. Lots of our modern swear-words used to be curses. For example, 'damn' is short for "may you be damned to hell". And you might think the word 'drat' is not a bad swear-word, but it comes from "God rot" – in other words, "may God rot you in hell". That's very scary indeed if you believe in hell and the power of curses ...

Do curses work?

Yes if ... you're afraid something bad will happen, you could make it happen by mistake. For example, someone might say you'd been cursed to fail an exam. You might believe this curse. You might be so scared that you wouldn't be able to think in the exam, so you might do badly!

Yes if ... you feel bad about something that you did, your feelings could make you more likely to be ill. Just like when you're scared.

Yes if ... you believe something bad will happen, you will notice more bad things round you. But someone who does not believe in the curse will just say, "Oh, that could have happened to anyone. It was nothing to do with the curse."

How a curse might work

The Choking Curse

What if a man is digging in his garden and he finds a box? He is about to open it when he sees some words. He brushes away the dirt and reads: "The person who opens this box will die a slow and horrible death. He will choke on his own tongue."

The man smiles. *What rubbish!* he thinks. He opens the box and inside finds gold, gold, and more gold. He will be rich! He begins to laugh. A large insect flies into his open mouth. In a panic, he tries to spit it out but first he feels a sharp sting. When he does spit it out he doesn't see it – he is dizzy with panic now. Perhaps it was a wasp. Will his tongue swell up? His throat? He reads those words again. His eyes open wide. His hand grips his throat. Now he believes the curse.

He gasps for breath. He chokes more. He can't breathe. He's dying. It must have been a wasp! His tongue must be swelling and the curse said he would die. In a panic, he presses the buttons of his mobile phone and dials 999.

As he becomes dizzier and dizzier, he feels a terrible pain in his chest. He puts his hand to his heart, his face twisting in agony. He knows this pain. He had a heart attack once before. The pain is like a knife. He can't breathe. He can't move. He can't scream. He falls on the ground. He can hear the faint sounds of an ambulance. It will be too late. By the time the ambulance arrives, his heart will have stopped.

He does not see that lying on the ground, dead, is just a small, black fly. Not a wasp at all.

Now, what if the man hadn't read the curse? He wouldn't have suddenly thought he'd been stung by a wasp and that his tongue was going to swell up. So he wouldn't have been scared. And if he hadn't been so scared, he wouldn't have had the heart attack. He might just have spat the fly out and got on with enjoying his gold.

So, could we say that the man only died because of the curse? If so ... curses work, don't they?

The Cursed Path

It's snowing and two boys, Jack and Paul, are hurrying home. If they're late, their parents will be angry. There's a short-cut they could take, but it goes past old Mr Brown's house, and they're not allowed along there. Adults don't like them going there because there's a fast river. The kids don't care about the river but they don't like Mr

Brown. He seems odd and a few years ago some kids said he'd put a curse on the path.

But Jack and Paul don't want to make their parents cross because they might be punished. They look at each other. "If we run fast, and don't make any noise, we'll be OK," says Paul. Jack nods and they set off. Fast. And silently.

But Mr Brown hears them and shouts something as they run. Jack and Paul feel cold shivers down their necks and they run faster. When they get to the end of the path, they are out of breath and scared. But they are safe.

They go on running. And they get home on time.

Next day at school, Jack falls when he is playing football and breaks his arm. At hospital, the nurses can't understand why he's so scared. "You're fine now, Jack," they say. But Jack has nightmares about Mr Brown for months.

He knows that the path was cursed.

Think about this: if the path was cursed, why wasn't Paul hurt as well? Could it just have been bad luck that Jack fell? How many people in your school have got hurt this year? Were they all victims of a curse? Also, if you investigated everyone who walked along any path, you might find that some of them had got hurt a few days later.

If there's a curse and someone gets hurt, does this have to mean that the curse made the accident? Couldn't it just have been bad luck?

Chapter 2

The Curse of the Mummy – King Tut

"Death shall come on swift wings to him who disturbs the peace of the King."

It is a hot day in Egypt. The year is 1922. A young British man called Howard Carter stands before a door-way, a closed door-way blocked up with huge rocks. He holds up his lamp and shadows flicker and dance on the walls.

He gazes at the stone above the door-way. Could he be wrong? No! The letters are clear to his expert eyes. This is the tomb of King Tut – Tutankhamun, the boy king from Ancient Egypt, who died more than 3,300 years ago.

Drops of sweat shine on Carter's forehead. He feels ill, and very tired. But he's excited too. He spent five years looking for this place and dreaming of this moment. There will be gold behind this door. Carter will be rich and famous. His heart is beating loudly.

But he mustn't smash open the door-way – not yet. Another man has paid for this trip and that man wants to be there at the moment when they enter the tomb. That other man is Lord Carnarvon. He is already rich but Lord Carnarvon is as keen as Carter to find the tomb of King Tut. He wants to be famous.

Carter runs his hand over the ancient wall. He turns his face and places his ear next to the cold stone. Can he hear anything? A slight buzzing of a mosquito, perhaps? They are deep underground. Could a mosquito come down this far? Perhaps his mind is just playing tricks ...

Only one other man has come with him down the passage-way. That man touches his arm now. "Come, master," he says. The man seems jumpy. All the workers are jumpy. They have heard that the tomb is cursed, like the tombs of many kings of Egypt. Anyone who tries to enter may be in danger from the curse.

Carter does not believe in curses. He tells himself that the buzzing is only in his head. He is dizzy with the heat and he is tired. And excited.

Touching the stone once more, feeling with his fingers the letters of King Tut's name, Carter turns and follows the man up to the open air.

Out in the bright sun-light, Carter is irritated by the men who are waiting for him. Some of them are excited – they know they will be paid more if they find the tomb. But others are angry – why should these British people dig up their holy places?

Many people are scared. They tell Carter that he must not break open the door. They say horrible dangers wait for him if he does. They talk of others who have broken open the doors of tombs and died soon afterwards. Powerful kings and powerful priests and very powerful magic that is now 3,000 years old.

"3,000 years old and dead as dust," says Carter. *These people don't know anything,* he tells himself. They know nothing of science – they are just full of silly stories.

Carter walks slowly towards his tent, hot, sweaty and tired out. He is looking forward to washing away the dirt and dust from his skin and hair. He is looking forward to a cool iced drink, before a meal cooked by his servants. Then he will write his diary and ...

But there is a noise, some shouting. Near his tent. What is happening? A man runs towards him, holding something in his hand. Someone else follows him. Other men and women stand in groups. They mutter and frown and all look at Carter. Now the man is there in front of him, holding out his hand.

On his hand is a bundle of yellow feathers. Horror grips Carter's heart. It is the yellow canary, the bird he brought from England. Dead. Twisted. Bloody. What has happened?

The man is speaking so fast that Carter can't understand him. Something about a

cobra. A holy snake. A cobra has been sent by ancient kings to warn Carter not to open the tomb. This is a curse, a warning. Death will come to anyone who dares ...

"Rubbish!" snaps Carter. "Where is the cobra? It must be killed before it kills us too!" And he orders the servants to hunt it down. Carter is not scared by such nonsense. A cobra is worth being afraid of, but a curse? Rubbish!

Three weeks later, Lord Carnarvon arrives in Egypt and the two men greet each other. They're excited. They hurry to the tomb. Four strong men stand guard outside. Not that anyone will dare enter it, not with all the talk of curses.

There are many stories, but the one that people seem to believe most is this: "Death shall come on swift wings to him who disturbs the peace of the King." People keep

looking up at the sky. Will it be an eagle?
A vulture?

Lord Carnarvon and Carter scramble
down the passage-way. They have no fear.
They are excited. Others follow, men who are
scared but are keen to be paid their reward.
The air down here is stale, dead. But it is nice
and cool and the heat of the day is left far
behind. Ancient dust floats in the light of
their lamps.

For a moment Carter thinks he hears that
buzzing again. But no! It must be his mind
playing tricks or perhaps a noise from
outside. The other men help him smash a
hole in the door-way of the tomb itself, but
Carter is the one who first looks in. Lord
Carnarvon holds his breath as Carter peers
through, holding his light in front of him.
"What do you see?" asks Lord Carnarvon.

"I see amazing, beautiful things!" says Carter, his eyes shining. Soon the hole is bigger and they can climb through.

Lord Carnarvon and Carter are the only two men who enter – the others have run away in terror. The two of them squeeze through the opening. They gasp, amazed at the gold, the cups and bowls, statues and coins. And there, lying in the middle of all this gold, is a stone tomb. Later they will find three golden coffins inside, fitting inside each other, and in the smallest they will find the body of the boy King Tut.

Lord Carnarvon and Carter can't believe their luck. Now, they will both be rich and famous, for ever!

****

Do they notice a small buzzing sound? Do they see a tiny flying insect?

Does Lord Carnarvon feel himself being bitten? If he does, does he ignore it?

After all, mosquito bites are common, aren't they?

And curses are just nonsense, of course ...

****

Some weeks later, Lord Carnarvon fell ill and died. Doctors weren't sure how he died, but it seemed that he had been bitten by an insect, and the bite had become infected.

And on the day he died, suddenly all the lights went out in Cairo, the capital of Egypt.

At home in England, his dog also died. Over the next few years, 21 of the people who had worked on the tomb died too.

And when, three years later, the mummy of King Tut was unwrapped, think of people's surprise when a tiny insect bite was found on the side of King Tut's face.

Just where Lord Carnarvon had been bitten.

Had Lord Carnarvon been the victim of the curse?

Or did he just die an unlucky death?

True or false? Curse or chance?

When you hear stories of a curse, some things are often exaggerated. Stories change each time they are told. And people love a good mystery, a bit of gossip. You know how when something strange happens at school, people tell each other the story, adding bits on, and suddenly the story contains lots of things that aren't true.

Look at the facts about King Tut's 'curse'. Newspapers said there were 21 deaths.

Lots of people didn't die till many years later – Carter, for a start. If there was a curse, why didn't he die too? Hundreds of men helped with the digging, and most didn't die then either!

26 people were there when the tomb was opened – only six of them died over the next 10 years. Scientists say that in fact, you would expect at least six people to die, because many of them weren't young. In fact, scientists have said that people connected to the tomb-opening had lived, on average, a year longer than normal …

No written curse was ever found. It was all just stories. Of course, stories can be true, but people say that someone made up part of the curse that everyone talked about.

A cobra killing a bird is not very surprising. Snakes are common in Egypt. And so are power cuts! Which was why all the lights went out in the city. And some people say that in fact the bird didn't die anyway. It's pretty impossible now to find out what was true and what wasn't. We don't know if the dog really died, either!

What about the other 21 deaths that the newspapers wrote about? Well, only six of the victims were at the tomb when it was opened. The others were just connected in some way to Lord Carnarvon or Carter or to one of the other people who were involved. If you include friends of friends, or the dog of a friend, then you'll find as many deaths as you want to find.

As for the mosquito bite mark on the mummy's face, there's no proof of a bite mark. A 3,000 year-old object is going to have small marks on it. If you want to believe it was a mosquito bite, then that's up to you ...

Chapter 3
Some Other Nasty Curses

Be careful with your curses ...

If you make a curse you might end up in danger yourself. Some people at the court of another king in Ancient Egypt called Rameses III, tried to curse him. They got a book of magic and made a powerful potion, using some of his hair, toe-nail clippings and pee that his wives had collected in secret. But their plot was found out and they were killed.

Cursing a rival

If you lived in Ancient Rome 2,000 years ago and you were about to have a race against someone, you might put a curse on that person. Ancient Romans wrote curses on bits of soft metal called lead, and threw them down a well. And of course, sometimes, your rival might wake up feeling sick. And then you'd believe your curse had worked.

Gypsy curses

Gypsies are travelling people who live in countries all round the world. Their way of life makes them seem very different from other people, so they have often been feared and treated badly. Even today, some people are scared of them, and there are lots of stories of gypsy curses.

I like this one about the gypsy curse and the football team. Up to 1946, Derby County had never won the FA Cup. Some people said

it was because their training ground was cursed by gypsies. (Others said it was because they were rubbish players!) Anyway, before the Cup Final in 1946, the team captain asked some other gypsies to get rid of the curse. "If you cross our palms with silver," they said. (They meant that they wanted money). So he gave them money and they got rid of the curse. The result? Derby County won 4 – 1.

The Curse of Superman

You know the *Superman* films? Well, people say they're cursed. Jerry Siegel and Joe Shuster were the writer and artist who invented the comic book character Superman in 1938. They were paid only 131 US dollars between them. When *Superman* later became a huge success, Siegel and Shuster weren't allowed to have any of the money that it

made. They were really angry (well you would be, wouldn't you). In 1975, they started to fight for their rights, and Shuster also wrote a letter, in which he cursed the film. In the end the film company agreed to pay a lot of money. Too late – the curse was there.

So, what happened? Well, lots of the actors did suffer disasters.

George Reeves (who played Superman in the 1951 film) killed himself.

Christopher Reeve (the most famous *Superman* actor) fell from a horse. He was so badly hurt that he could not move his body below his neck. He died 10 years later. His wife died of lung cancer (though she did not smoke) aged 44.

Richard Pryor (who acted in *Superman III* in 1983) got an illness called multiple sclerosis and died of a heart attack.

Marlon Brando (who played Superman's father in *Superman* in 1978) had a son who was sent to prison for 10 years for killing his sister's lover. She killed herself soon afterwards.

Lee Quigley (who was the baby in *Superman* in 1978) died aged 14 from taking drugs.

Kate Bosworth (who was in the film *Superman Returns* in 2006) blamed the curse for her break-up with the actor Orlando Bloom. And another *Superman* actor, Brandon Routh, had a motorbike crash ...

There are lots of other examples. Some actors, such as Ashton Kutcher, say they turned down parts in *Superman* films, because of the curse.

Mind you, the films and TV shows have made a fortune for the company that owns them. Not so cursed, then? It is odd that the 'curse' seems only to affect the actors who play good guys in the films. Nothing bad happened to actors like Gene Hackman or Terence Stamp, who played the bad guys!

Family Curses

There are many old stories of families where a curse seems to carry on for the children and grand-children and great-grand-children. Sometimes the story is that a god is angry about something. Sometimes bad things keep happening to a family, so people say, "Oh they must be cursed. Maybe it's because old Sir Jack stole some land in 1542." Sometimes members of a family keep getting the same illness. We now know how genes are passed from parents to children, but long ago people just thought of curses. Here is an example of each of these things.

The Curse of Oedipus

This is a famous story from ancient Greece. We don't know if any of it's true, but it's a great story. The gods cursed King Laius because he kidnapped a young man, who then killed himself. The curse was that if Laius had a son, the son would kill him. So, when Laius and his wife, Jocasta, had a son, Laius took the baby to the mountains and left him there. He put a wooden stake through his foot to keep him there (as though he was going anywhere!). Anyway, a shepherd rescued the baby and he grew up safely. No one knew that he was Laius' son. He was called Oedipus, which means 'swollen foot'.

When Oedipus grew up, an oracle (like a fortune-teller) said he would kill his father and marry his mother. Remember that Oedipus thought his parents were the people he had grown up with, so he left home, because he loved them and didn't want to hurt them in any way. On his journey, he had a fight with a stranger and killed him. (It sounds like an early example of road rage!) The sad truth was that the man was Laius, his real father. So the first part of the curse had come true.

To cut a long story short, he married Jocasta, not knowing that she was in fact his mother. So, that was the second part of the curse. But the curse went on. Jocasta killed herself when she found out she'd married her son. Oedipus blinded himself by poking his eyes out *(ow!)*. Then the curse fell on his daughters, and only when every member of his family was dead was the curse finished.

The Kennedy Family Curse

The Kennedy family is one of the most powerful families in the history of America. But they have had many disasters.

John F Kennedy (known as JFK) was elected President of the United States in 1960. He was shot dead in 1963. His baby son Patrick had died three months earlier. Another son, called John Junior, died in a plane crash, aged 38.

JFK's older brother, Joseph, also died in a plane crash, aged 29. His sister, Kathleen, died in another plane crash aged 28. Another brother, Robert (Bobby), was shot dead in 1968. And yet another brother, Edward (Ted), drove a car off a bridge in 1969. He didn't die but the woman with him in the car drowned.

Five of Bobby's seven sons met with disaster. Joseph was in a car crash that left one person paralysed. Robert Jr had drug problems, as did a younger brother, David, who died from taking drugs. Edward had a leg cut off, aged 12. Michael died in a skiing accident, aged 39.

Ted's son Patrick was treated for drug abuse.

****

Cursed or not cursed? The Kennedys led very risky lives. Being President of the United

States is risky! Drugs and alcohol can kill you. As a rich family, they had their own planes and may not always have followed good flying rules. Skiing and fast driving are also risky. And it was a huge family, and just as many members of the family had happy, long lives.

What do you think?

Dying to Sleep

There are lots of stories from history where a family seems to be cursed by an illness that keeps being passed on from parents to children. We know that this is because of things called genes. If a mother or father has the gene for a particular thing, such as brown eyes, or artistic talent or an illness, the gene may pass to a child.

So, an illness that gets passed on in families is not a strange magic curse, but something we can explain (and sometimes cure).

A very sad example of this is a family from Italy that had a terrible and very rare illness called Fatal Familial Insomnia. For 200 years this illness was passed from parents to children in this family. The illness starts in middle-age, and the person who has it can't sleep. Not at all. Not even a bit. At the moment there is no cure. For many years, the family must have seemed cursed by a strange illness, but we now know that they simply had a bad gene, which they were passing to some of their children.

It is lucky that this illness is very rare indeed. At the moment, there are only about 27 families in the world who seem to be affected and only some family members become ill.

Chapter 4
The Curse of Carlisle

It is a cold night in the city of Carlisle, in the North of England. The year is 2005. In a gloomy under-pass near a museum, stands a huge rock that weighs 14 tonnes. There are 383 words carved into its side. The words are part of a powerful curse, first spoken nearly 500 years ago. The curse can't still have any power, can it? Not now?

The curse used to be much longer, made up of 1,096 words in total. It was first made by a very important man of the church, an archbishop. He wrote the curse to stop robbers from stealing the sheep on the land round Carlisle. The words sound powerful and horrible.

I curse their head and all the hairs of their head. I curse their face, their brain, their mouth, their nose, their tongue, their teeth, their forehead, their shoulders, their breast, their heart, their stomach, their back, their womb, their arms, their legs, their hands, their feet, and every part of their body, from the top of their head to the soles of their feet, before and behind, within and without ... And, finally, I condemn them forever to the deep pit of hell, there to remain with the Devil ... and their bodies to the gallows of Burrow Moor, first to be hanged, then ripped and torn by dogs, pigs, and other wild beasts, hated by all the world.

In 2001 the Council paid an artist to carve some of these words onto a rock so that everyone could see it. They thought that tourists and locals might be interested.

But not everyone is happy. Suddenly, bad luck has struck the town. There has been a horrible murder of a baby. All the sheep and cows nearby have been killed by foot and mouth disease. Terrible flooding has destroyed homes and shops. A huge fire has destroyed property. Some even blamed the curse for Carlisle United football team losing all its games.

The Council is discussing the problem. Should they remove the stone and destroy it? But they had paid thousands of pounds to the artist. Money will be wasted and the artist will be angry. And all because some people believe an ancient curse.

But many people do believe it. A local vicar has said that the curse is a deadly weapon. Other people have begged for it to be taken away. And the curse was made by an archbishop, a powerful man of God. Now the Bishop of Carlisle has said, "Words carry power to affect those who read them."

There are even stories that some men who set up the stone have died ...

After several meetings and much talking with local people, the Council decided ... the stone will stay. It would be silly to destroy it, they say. People would laugh at us if we did.

And so, in a dark under-pass, the Carlisle Stone still stands, its words cold and strong.

****

Do you believe the bad things happened because of the curse? What would you have said if you'd been at the meetings? Can you believe what you want to believe? Which is more powerful – you or a curse?

Chapter 5

Why Do We Believe What We Believe?

Everyone is different. Some people believe more easily than others. It depends on what sort of person you are.

Some people don't believe in weird things at all. They are called sceptics. They say there's always a sensible scientific reason for everything – even if they can't say what the reason is. Sceptics like to say "Rubbish!" a lot.

Some people believe in everything like ghosts, magic and curses. They like the idea of weird things happening and they are happy not to have science explaining everything with a boring reason.

Some people are half-way between. They think that most things have scientific reasons but that there might be something weird out there as well.

Even in the modern world where we look for scientific reasons for everything, many of us like to believe there might still be mystery. I think that's why we like stories. In a way, we like some things not to be explained.

Do you believe in curses?

So, what do you believe? Do you think that curses only have power if people are scared of them? Or do you think there's really some strange magic that can make curses come true?

If you found a box of gold with a curse written on it, would you open the box? And then if an insect flew into your mouth, and you felt a sting ...

AUTHOR CHECK LIST

Nicola Morgan

Who do you think is the scariest villain from history?

All villains are scary to me because I am a total wimp. But I'm only scared of them in the same way as I'm scared of snakes – I don't respect villains at all. I think they're disgusting people.

If you could time travel, what period of history would you like to visit? And why?

I'd rather live today than at any other time in history. So, if I could time-travel, I wouldn't. Living in this time, in this country, we are very very lucky – medicines, comfort, things to make our lives easier, we're able to say what we feel and not be put in prison for it – a society where everyone is seen as valuable. (Except villains).

What are you scared of?

Not doing as much as I can with my life, my friends and family dying, caves. Lots of other things too, but you haven't got all day!

What inspired you to write a book on curses?

Barrington Stoke asked me to write a book about something I was interested in. And right then it was curses because I was writing a novel about a curse.

ILLUSTRATOR CHECK LIST

Kevin Hopgood

Do you believe in the power of curses?

I'm far too rational to believe in the power of curses.
However, I will avoid walking under a ladder, so maybe
I'm not as rational as I like to think ...

**Apart from the ones in the book, what's the most unusual
curse you have heard of?**

"Hear this, thou breaker of the commandments, for you
will be thrown into a den of hyperactive lions!"

**If you could put a curse on anyone, who would it be?
And why?**

I'd like to put a curse on whoever created the *Teletubbies*
– for making a programme that children love but that's
completely mind-numbing for their parents!

What kind of curse would you put on them? And why?

I can't think of a curse painful and horrific enough for
such a crime. Needless to say it would hurt a lot ...

**Of all the curses in the book, which would you least like
to have placed on you. And why?**

I've drawn for American superhero comics in the past, so
I'd be wary of the curse of Superman if I ever got to draw
him ...

Barrington Stoke would like to thank all its readers for commenting on the manuscript before publication and in particular:

Anton
Kathryn Hagar
Sheena Hagar
Marta Kukurowska
Luke McDonagh
Paulina Nicewicz
Cameron Stuart

Become a Consultant!

Would you like to give us feedback on our titles before they are published? Contact us at the email address below – we'd love to hear from you!

info@barringtonstoke.co.uk
www.barringtonstoke.co.uk

Try another book in the

REALITY CHECK

series

The Land of Whizzing Arrows
by Simon Chapman

Pocket Hero
by Pippa Goodhart

The Last Duel
by Martyn Beardsley

Escape from Colditz
by Deborah Chancellor

All available from our website:
www.barringtonstoke.co.uk